D0936223

A SHORT HISTORY OF
GLASS
ENGRAVING

A SHORT HISTORY OF
GLASS
ENGRAVING

BY PAUL N. PERROT

Assistant Secretary for Museum Programs,
Smithsonian Institution
and
Former Director, The Corning Museum of Glass

STEUBEN GLASS · NEW YORK

LIBRARY OF THE
MUSEUM OF FINE ARTS

Copyright © 1973 by Steuben Glass
a Division of Corning Glass Works
International Standard Book Number 0–911442–06–5
Library of Congress Catalog Card Number 73–82156
Printed in The United States of America

LIBRARY OF THE
MUSEUM OF FINE ARTS

To the engravers of Steuben Glass, 1933-1973

JOSEPH CARROLL
FREDERICK DUDLEY
ROLAND ERLACHER
PAUL GRIEFF
LADISLAV HAVLIK
ROGER KEAGLE
ANTHONY KELLER
ANTON KRALL
JOSEPH LIBISCH
THOMAS MILLER
CLEMENT NITSCHE
JOSEPH OVESZNEY
EDWARD PALME, JR.
REINHART RAABE
LUBOMIR RICHTER
PETER SCHELLING
ROGER SELANDER
KENNETH VAN ETTEN

Three centuries have produced many masters of copper wheel engraving. If now Steuben, by its contributions and example, can help to sustain both interest in and practice of this delicate art of decoration, it will feel well rewarded.

NK5106
P46
1974

CONTENTS

ACKNOWLEDGMENTS

Steuben Glass acknowledges with gratitude permission to reproduce photographs of pieces from the collections of:

THE CORNING MUSEUM OF GLASS
THE METROPOLITAN MUSEUM OF ART
THE ORREFORS MUSEUM
STAATLICHE KUNSTSAMMLUNGEN KASSEL
UMELECKOPRUMYSLOVE MUZEUM

BRADY HILL COMPANY
JEROME STRAUSS

I. THE TECHNIQUES

In spite of its apparent hardness, glass can be fairly easily cut or engraved. This property was recognized early in the history of the material and throughout the last 3,500 years it has been exploited for either utilitarian or ornamental purposes by virtually all of the cultures that have manufactured glass.

The earliest method consisted of scratching the surface with a sharp point of natural stone, hard metal or, in recent centuries, a diamond. But other ways were also found to abrade the glass, including turning on a lathe and cutting with rotating stone wheels; the rough grooves ground into the surface of the glass were often polished to a smooth, brilliant finish. These methods were generally used to create large geometric decoration. Engraving, on the other hand, was employed to create smaller, more detailed designs. It was done with small stone wheels which rotated on a spindle and were lubricated with water. In the hands of a skillful craftsman, this method produced intricate, though somewhat rough, designs. Copper wheel engraving was the last refinement in the abrasive techniques: copper discs of various thicknesses, diameters and rim profiles were rotated individually on a spindle; from time to time, an abrasive such as emery (now carborundum) mixed with oil was applied by the craftsman to the face of the wheel. Pressed against the vessel or other object by the rotating wheel, the abrasive ground its way into the surface, the roughness of the cut being

determined by the coarseness of the abrasive, the
depth and width of the cut by the size of the wheel. It
is this technique which, since the early 17th century,
has produced the most refined and detailed glass
engraving. Basic methods have changed little over the
last 350 years, and apart from the substitution of elec-
tricity for foot or "little boy" power, the use of ball
bearings and a few other lesser changes, a 17th century

FIG. 1: *A glass engraver. Woodcut, probably by Christopher Weigel. Germany, Nuremberg, late 17th century. Collection The Corning Museum of
Glass.*

engraver would be quite at home with the most advanced 20th century glass engraving equipment (Figs. 1 — 2).

The art of copper wheel engraving has been preserved. It is one of the most successful decorative techniques of Steuben Glass, the skill of whose craftsmen reflects the centuries of experimentation and tradition summarized in the following pages.

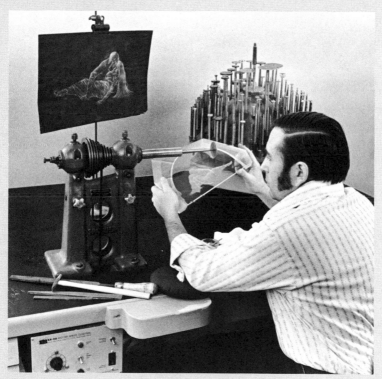

FIG. 2: *A Steuben Glass engraver, Roland Erlacher. United States, Corning, 1973.*

II. ENGRAVING
IN ANCIENT TIMES

One of the first datable engraved vessels is a goblet, now in the collection of The Metropolitan Museum of Art, New York, bearing the incised cartouche of Thutmose III, who reigned in Egypt from 1504 to 1450 B.C. (Fig. 3). Later, in Mesopotamia, during the reign of Sargon II from 722 to 705 B.C., the cutting, grinding and polishing of glass reached an extraordinarily sophisticated state of development. It is from this period onward that lapidary techniques became prominent in glass. Superb work was done for the rulers of Achaemenid Persia, and the tradition continued into Hellenistic time. Cutting and engraving as we know it today flourished during the Roman period (Fig. 4). The art reached a high point with the cameo glasses of the Augustan age, the best example being the Portland vase, now in the British Museum. Later, in the 4th century A.D., the tour de force aspect of cameo carving was surpassed in the diatreta — intricate, lace-like, undercut vessels made in north Italy and the Rhineland.

These decorative techniques remained popular in the Near East and continued to thrive long after the Roman Empire had fallen. The engraved glasses of the Islamic period are particularly notable for the unity between form and decoration and, indeed, some were so superbly conceived and executed that they remain unsurpassed.

FIG. 3: *Goblet bearing the name of Thut-mose III. Egypt, XVIII Dynas-
ty, about 1490 B.C. Height, as restored, 5-1/8". Turquoise blue glass with
gold rims at lip and foot (which is restored). Collection The Metropolitan
Museum of Art, Bequest of Lord Carnarvon, 1923.*

FIG. 4: *Fragment of bowl. Deep reddish-purple glass, wheel incised. Roman Empire, 3rd-4th century A.D. Maximum width 3". Collection The Corning Museum of Glass.*

III. THE RENAISSANCE
AND EARLY 18TH CENTURY
ENGRAVING

In western Europe, the engraving of glass waned with the passing of Roman order and did not reappear as a notable artistic manifestation before the high Renaissance. Lapidary techniques, however, were used on transparent quartz, which was cut and engraved from Carolingian times onward into the Middle Ages. This natural stone, also known as rock crystal, was used extensively in the 14th, 15th and 16th centuries for the making of all sorts of decorative or ritualistic vessels. They were carved from massive blocks, clear and often flawless, and engraved much as glass is today. North Italy and Bohemia, by the 16th century, were the two predominant centers of production.

The skill involved was enormous, for this hard substance had to be entirely hollowed out and the vessels formed and polished before the final engraved decoration could be executed. The difficulty of the technique and the extensive labor and time required, as well as the gradual shrinking of the available supply of raw material, forced rock crystal carvers, toward the latter part of the 16th century, to seek new materials. This search seems to have occurred primarily in southern Germany and Bohemia and to have reached a solution by the beginning of the 17th century when Caspar Lehmann, an engraver at the court of Emperor Rudolph II, was given a privilege for engraving glass (Figs. 5-6). Lehmann's work was amazing in its sponta-

FIG. 5: *Beaker engraved by Caspar Lehmann after Johann Sadeler's copper plate engraving "Allegory of Liberality, Nobility and Power." Bohemia, Prague, dated "1605." Height 8-13/16". Made for State Counsellor Wolf Sigismund of Losenstein and his wife, the Lady Susanna of Rogendorf. Signed "C. Lehman." Collection Uměleckoprůmyslové muzeum, Prague.*

FIG. 6: *Detail of Fig. 5. "Liberality."*

neity and vigor. Perhaps no one since has excelled him in rendering plant formations, butterflies and insects in as lively and crisp a fashion.

Caspar Lehmann had many followers, particularly in the region of Nuremberg where extensive glass engraving workshops were established by the middle of the 17th century. These centers produced superb vessels embellished with narrative scenes (Figs. 7-8),

FIG. 7

FIG. 7: *Goblet engraved with a boar-hunting scene. Germany, Nuremberg, about 1660-1670. Height 11-3/16". Collection The Corning Museum
of Glass.*

FIG. 8: *Detail of Fig. 7. The kill.*

portraits, cityscapes and commemorative inscriptions, all done with great precision and yet having the direct freshness of works which are originally conceived rather than copied. By the end of the 17th century the Germanic lands were producing elaborate cut and engraved glass: the workshops of Potsdam (Figs. 9-10)

FIG. 9

FIG. 9: *Covered beaker probably engraved by Gottfried Spiller. Germany, Potsdam, about 1700. Height 8 - 5/8". The concave medallion, flanked by putti, is engraved with the monogram of Elector Frederick III of Brandenburg. Collection The Corning Museum of Glass.*

FIG. 10: *Detail of Fig. 9. Putto with palm fronds.*

and Nuremberg, in Germany, and numerous communities in Bohemia and Silesia (Figs. 11-12) were vying with one another in combining intaglio and relief engraving, creating highly three dimensional effects of depth and relief. The emphasis on abrasive techniques at this period was such that the skill of the glassmaker was often completely obscured by the work of the engraver.

Many other important glassmaking centers became notable in the 18th century. Franz Gundelach of Kassel, Germany (Fig. 13), carved and engraved his glass with a boldness matched by few of his contemporaries. Others, such as Georg Friedrich Killinger of Nuremberg (Figs. 14-15), executed delicate landscapes with superbly rendered architectural details and, on other vessels, elaborate coats of arms surrounded by wreaths, often with inscriptions and an array of decorative motifs typical of the period.

FIG. 11: *Goblet with a portrait of Augustus the Strong. Possibly engraved by Friedrich Winter. Bohemia or Silesia, about 1700. Height 13-1/2". Collection The Corning Museum of Glass.*

FIG. II

FIG. 12: *Detail of Fig. 11.*

FIG. 13: *Medallion with the head of a philosopher. Engraved by Franz Gundelach. Germany, Kassel, about 1710-1716. Diameter 9-13/16". Collection Staatliche Kunstsammlungen Kassel, Kassel.*

FIG. 14: *Covered goblet with a pastoral scene including ruins and a battle. Engraved by Georg Friedrich Killinger. Germany, Nuremberg, about 1710-1720. Total height 13-1/2".* *Collection Jerome Strauss.*

FIG. 15: *Detail of Fig. 14. The battle.*

IV. LATE 18TH AND 19TH CENTURY ENGRAVING

Germany and Bohemia remained the centers of glass engraving during the latter part of the 18th and throughout much of the 19th century. In 1800 Dominik Biemann, one of the greatest engravers of all time, was born in Harrachov, Bohemia. He studied both physiology and phrenology, and his portraits, executed between the 1820's and the 1850's, are notable for their high degree of finish, psychological insight and remarkable understanding of facial anatomy (Figs. 16-17).

FIG. 16

FIG. 16: *Portrait plaque of an unknown man. Engraved by Dominik Biemann. Bohemia, Prague, dated "1834." Diameter 3-3/4". Signed "D. Bimann." Collection The Corning Museum of Glass.*

FIG. 17: *Detail of Fig. 16.*

During the 19th century engraving in the Bohemian style was a favorite decorative technique in western Europe, Britain and the United States. Bohemian and German glass engravers migrated to other countries, particularly to England where they produced brilliant works exploiting the high quality of the lead glass which was made by British glassmakers. English lead "crystal" was especially suited to the abrasive technique since it was softer than the potash lime glass generally in use on the Continent. William Fritsche, a Bohemian who worked for Thomas Webb & Sons in Stourbridge, was a leading artist-engraver. The ewer in Figs. 18 and 19 is one of his masterpieces.

FIG. 18: *Ewer, cut and engraved by William Fritsche. England, Stourbridge, Thomas Webb & Sons, dated "1886." Height 15-1/8". Signed "W. Fritsche Stourbridge." Collection The Corning Museum of Glass.*

(Page 34) FIG. 19: *Detail of Fig. 18. Head of Neptune, at neck of ewer.*

FIG. 18

V. ENGRAVING
IN THE 20TH CENTURY

In the latter part of the 19th century and the early part of the 20th, Bohemia continued to be a leading center for engraved glass of high quality. The firm of Lobmeyr was particularly noted for its exacting standards and for providing its skilled engravers with designs produced by leading contemporary artists such as Michael Powolny (Figs. 20-21).

The standards achieved by that firm, and by other Central European glass factories, were an inspiration to Sweden's Orrefors Glassworks; during World War I the firm hired two artists, Edvard Hald and Simon Gate. They introduced new concepts of glass design which were to have a tremendous influence on the subsequent development of European and American glass (Figs. 22-23).

In the United States, Steuben Glass, founded in 1903 by Thomas G. Hawkes and Frederick Carder in Corning, New York, continued Bohemian-English decorative engraving while introducing colorful glasses in the Art Nouveau style. The company was acquired in 1918 by Corning Glass Works and became its Steuben division. In 1933 young Arthur A. Houghton, Jr., a great-grandson of the founder of Corning Glass Works, reorganized the Steuben division. The firm discontinued the production of colored glass and adopted a fine quality high-lead-content optical glass of great clarity which has been its distinguishing characteristic ever since.

FIG. 20: *Beaker, Good Fortune—Health—Joy, designed by Michael Powolny;
engraved by Max Rössler. Austria, Vienna, J.&L. Lobmeyr. 1917. Height 5-1/4".
Signed "MR." Collection The Corning Museum of Glass.*

FIG. 21: *Detail of Fig. 20. Joy.*

FIG. 22: *The Ox Heads designed by Simon Gate; engraved by Gustav Abels.
Sweden, Orrefors, dated "1923." Height 16". Signed "Simon Gate — Orrefors — Gustav Abels." Covered urn engraved with four scenes separated by figures in column
form. Ox heads are engraved on the cover. Collection The Orrefors Museum.*

FIG. 23: *Detail of Fig. 22. A dancer.*

Having this brilliant glass, eminently suited to engraving, Steuben drew from a long tradition and used the talents of craftsmen trained in the United States and abroad who, collectively, could do virtually anything with the rotating copper wheel.

FIG. 24: *Gazelle Bowl designed by Sidney Waugh; engraved by Joseph Libisch. United States, Corning, Steuben Glass, 1935. Diameter 6-1/2". Signed "Sidney Waugh." Collection The Metropolitan Museum of Art, Purchase, 1935, Edward C. Moore, Jr., Gift Fund.*

The Gazelle Bowl (Figs. 24-25) was its first major piece and the first of some one hundred fifty designs for glass engraving by the sculptor Sidney Waugh. The bowl is still being executed on commission. Over the years Steuben has produced more than five hundred different engraved pieces, with emphasis on figurative rather than purely decorative designs and with con-

FIG. 25: *Detail of Fig. 24. Gazelles.*

tinually increasing demands on the skill of the engravers. The work being done today is technically superior to that of only a few years ago. Figures 26-33 represent recent major works done by four of the firm's seven fine arts engravers.

FIG. 26

FIG. 26: *The Butterfly designed by George Thompson; engraving design by Alexander Seidel; engraved by Ladislav Havlik. United States, Corning, Steuben Glass, 1967. Height 8". Prism engraved with the body and single wing of a butterfly. The second wing is a reflection, opening or closing according to the angle of view. Private collections.*

FIG. 27: *Detail of Fig. 26. The butterfly.*

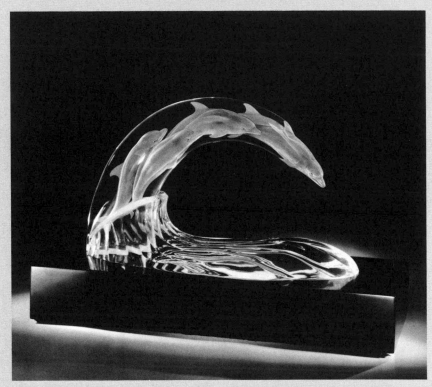

FIG. 28: *Sea Chase designed by Lloyd Atkins; engraved by Peter Schelling. United States, Corning, Steuben Glass, 1969. Length, excluding base, 13-1/2". Private collections.*

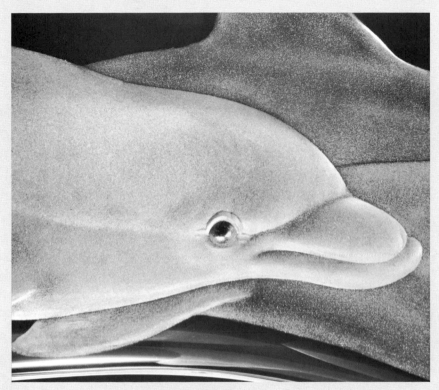

FIG. 29: *Detail of Fig. 28. Head of a dolphin.*

FIG. 30: *Dandelions designed by Paul Schulze; engraving design by Donald Crowley; engraved by Kenneth Van Etten. United States, Corning, Steuben Glass, 1972. Height 7". Prism engraved with a dandelion cluster. By refracted image, the plant appears to divide and multiply as the viewer's position changes. Private collections.*

FIG. 31: *Detail of Fig. 30. Seed head drawn by diamond point.*

FIG. 32: *The Myth of Adonis designed by Donald Pollard; engraving design by Jerry Pfohl; engraved by Roland Erlacher; goldwork by Cartier, Inc. United States, Corning, Steuben Glass, 1966. Height 6 - 7/8".* *Casket representing the life, death and rebirth of Adonis, symbol of the seed of life. Mounted in 18 karat gold. Collection Brady Hill Company, Birmingham, Michigan.*

FIG. 33: *Detail of Fig. 32. Head of Zeus.*

Unlike most venerable traditions, the art of wheel engraving continues at a level of technical excellence worthy of its greatest masters. A persistent attachment to this most difficult, expensive and rewarding of techniques has made Steuben, today, the uncontested leader in contemporary glass engraving.